MW00366951

To

_____

From

_____

© 2000 by Bruce Bickel and Stan Jantz

ISBN 1-57748-889-X

Cover art: Debra Dixon

Published by Promise Press, an imprint of Barbour Publishing, Inc., P.O. Box 719, Uhrichsville, Ohio 44683
http://www.barbourbooks.com

Member of the
Evangelical Christian
Publishers Association

Printed in China.

GOD IS IN THE
SMALL STUFF
for DADS

BRUCE & STAN

Happy
B-day
Allen, We
You are the
greatest
son-in-law!
Mom + Dad

PROMISE
PRESS
An imprint of Barbour Publishing

FAMILY HERITAGE

You might have a godly heritage, which is something to be thankful for. Investigate it. Did your ancestors struggle for their religious freedom? Was one of your ancestors of the same name involved in some noble cause that left its mark? Dig up the details and talk about them with your children. Tell them the stories of their name.

When it comes to your name—whether it's your first or your last—you can either ignore it or live up to it. And if there isn't much to live up to, then determine to be the first in your family to bring honor to the family name.

~

Instead of finances, make your greatest gift to your children a rich heritage of personal qualities such as integrity, joy, and spiritual sensitivity to God. Devote your time, energy, and creativity to teaching and modeling such qualities to your children. This is the most valuable legacy you can leave to your children (and it is tax-free, too).

Make an effort to remember God's continual provision for your family. When you do, something interesting will happen. The more you remember what God has done in your lives in the past, the more you will see Him at work in your lives in the present.

~

*If you are having a
difficult time
being thankful,
the problem may be
your memory.*

$\mathcal{The}$ most personal spiritual celebration you can observe is the spiritual birthday of each family member. Can you imagine the effectiveness of a spiritual birthday celebration on children and teenagers in your family? As you affirm God's place in their lives, God will bless them as individuals and your family as a whole. God enjoys the praises of His people, especially when we tell Him how much we value what He has done for us.

~

We are to love God wholeheartedly and teach our children to do the same. That's the kind of legacy that will last for generations and please God into eternity.

Live your life so that when you die, people will know that you

- loved others clearly.
- loved your family dearly.
- loved God completely.

Hear, O Israel!
The Lord is our God,
the Lord alone.
And you must love the Lord
your God with all your heart,
all your soul, and all your strength.
And you must commit yourselves
wholeheartedly to these commands
I am giving you today.
Repeat them again and again
to your children.

DEUTERONOMY 6:4–7 NLT

THE
SPIRITUAL
FAMILY

Your family can experience the real and living God, but you must approach this relationship like others you value. You can't expect to develop a close friendship with someone whom you totally ignore. You need to acknowledge God's presence, recognize His activity in your lives, and appreciate His provisions. Stated simply: You need to make room for God in your lives. When you do, you'll see God's hand directing you, you'll hear His voice comforting you, you'll sense His spirit embracing you. He will be real to you.

15

$\mathcal{The}$ simple exercise
of praying together
regularly as a fam-
ily will do more
to strengthen
your family
than any-
thing else
you could do
together.

*Prayer
is a privilege.
Don't take it for
granted.*

Reading the Bible is not drudgery when you understand what you are reading. It should be part of the daily routine for each member of your family. Between the covers of that sacred book is the information God wants you to know each day: Personal information about you and for you, written by the One who knows you best.

~

The Bible will find you
where you are,
and it will show you
where you ought to go.

FAMILY
FUN

Okay, so managing a family is serious business. That doesn't mean that you have to be serious, too. Refuse to succumb to your naturally negative tendencies. Rise above the rigor—if not the responsibility—of running your household and have some fun. Accent your routine with some family recreation.

~

~

There are two kinds
of recreation:
planned and spontaneous.
Make time for both.

~

Recreation doesn't have to be expensive. Too many of us think we have to spend a lot of money on fancy sports equipment or elaborate vacations in order to have fun. Wrong thinking! Enjoy the natural world that God created for us in the first place. God is delighted when we enjoy His created things: lakes, forests, the mountains, the ocean, the countryside. . .

~

Above all else,
guard your heart,
for it affects
everything you do.

PROVERBS 4:23 NLT

Everything you let in through your heart's gate affects who you are and what you do. If you are a spiritually maturing person, you will post a guard that says, "Stop! Who goes there?" to the infotainment knocking relentlessly at your heart's door. If that part of your life isn't important to you—or you don't know any better—then your heart is like a Denny's restaurant: *always open.*

~

~

As a gatekeeper—
to your heart and
to your home—
you can never
let your guard down.

~

Right living starts with right thinking, which is another way to look at wisdom. That's why the Bible says:

Fix your thoughts on what is true and honorable and right. Think about things that are pure and lovely and admirable. Think about things that are excellent and worthy of praise.

PHILIPPIANS 4:8 NLT

Think about the transformation that can occur in your marriage if you both attempt to be God's servant to each other. No longer will your marriage be characterized by vicious sarcasm or ridicule. Instead, each of you will be looking for opportunities to help the other.

~

~

Try to see yourself
and your spouse from
God's perspective.
It will change
the way that you live.
It will change
the way you love.

~

The more we view God as a
provider—and teach our children to
do the same—the more we will see
that nothing is too small for His
involvement. We will stop taking for
granted our daily provisions and the
small pleasures our family enjoys,
and begin to see them all as coming
from God.

~

Whether you're flipping burgers or writing computer code, you have the opportunity every day to show your boss, your coworkers, and your subordinates just how much God matters to you. And the best way to do that is to work to the best of your ability with the highest integrity every single day.

~

For many people the heavy responsibilities of home and family and earning a living absorb all their time and strength. Yet such a home—where love is—may be a light shining in a dark place, a silent witness to the reality and the love of God.

OLIVE WYON

~

After a
busy season at work,
schedule a weekend away
or a mini-vacation
with your family.

FAMILY
CHALLENGES

Just as difficult times can unite you with your family, a crisis may be the event that reconnects you with God. He often gets forgotten in the "good times" when you are thinking that you are self-sufficient. But when the money runs out, or your health is in jeopardy, or the children are in trouble, you can turn to God and He will be there. No appointment necessary. You don't have to take a number. And you won't get stuck with His voice mail. You can speak directly to Him, and He can make Himself known to you.

$\mathcal{W}e$ have a God who is in the business of restoring relationships. The most important relationship is ours with Him. While we can reject Him quickly and frequently, He is always ready to forgive and receive us back into fellowship with Him. He never abandons us. He never quits on us. He never gives up on us.

God's unconditional love is the

model He wants
us to use for
marriage. So,
in our age of
disposability,
let's not look at
marriage as
something that
can be discarded
or recycled.

37

When you consider that God has the events in your life under His watchful eye, you realize that He can bring into your life the things that you need to learn. Of course, you need to be living life with the expectation of learning from it. Look at life as an opportunity to obtain the education that God has in store for you. After all, what you learn in life is tuition-free.

~

In every new and difficult situation, ask yourself: "What can I learn from this?"

You can talk about what is important to you, but your true priorities will be revealed by how you handle your finances. And those around you may not pay attention to what you are saying, but they will certainly notice how you spend your money.

*Whatever your
treasure is,
there your heart and
thought will also be.*

MATTHEW 6:21 NLT

FAMILY
RESPONSIBILITY

Here's a suggestion on how to gain the respect of everyone around you: Show ultimate respect for God. Who else in your life is worthy of more honor and praise than the One who created you, the One who loves you, and the One who knows you better than anyone? As you show respect for God in how you talk about Him, how you express your love for Him, how you read His Word, and how you pray to Him, you will encourage others in your family to do the same.

~

*Like all moral values,
respect is caught
more than it is taught.*

You earn respect as a parent by having high regard for your children. As you care for them, keep them safe, teach them, and love them unconditionally, you will gain the respect of your kids. There will be no yelling, no demanding, no competition. . . .

~

Responsibility is a character trait that will produce strong families (and a strong society). But responsibility doesn't happen by accident. It isn't acquired from a parent's wishful thinking or good intentions. Responsibility comes as the result of years of character training. It is developed gradually. If it is not nurtured in your home, you will be stunting your child's growth.

~

Few things help an individual
more than to
place responsibility upon him
and to let him know that
you trust him.

BOOKER T. WASHINGTON

Take heart!
Your consistent,
loving discipline will
ultimately teach your children
to discipline themselves.
Then your job will be easier.

~

Early discipline
averts
future disaster.

Listening communicates to others in the family that you really care about them. Make no mistake about it. Listening, like all forms of effective communication, takes effort. Listening is work. But the results can be incredible.

~

It was hard to have
a conversation
with anyone.
There were too many
people talking.

YOGI BERRA

When God is the authority in the home, your family can be a partnership of equals. Oh, sure, the husband, wife, and children will have different roles, but they can trust each other, knowing that each person functions in the family under God's leadership and authority.

~

*Some people
handle authority well
and grow in the process;
others misuse authority
and just over-inflate.*

You should protect your children from many things, but don't protect them so much that they miss the opportunity to make decisions. Decision-making is a skill that must be developed. And part of the learning process includes making a few wrong decisions. Isn't it better to allow your children to make a few "wrong decisions" when the

consequences are relatively minor
and you are around to
assist in the learn-
ing process?
Don't let your
children's first
confrontation
and struggle with
major decisions
come after they have left home.

Including your children in the process is the best method to teach them decision-making, but the most important principle to teach them about decision-making is to include God in the process. Don't let them think that God is only interested in the major decisions of life. Show them that God is interested in the smallest details of our lives.

~

~

Freedom is the ability to make decisions. Wisdom is the ability to make the right decisions.

~

Living a life of good spiritual choices isn't easy, but God has given us the two most important tools we need: His Word and prayer. When you read the Bible, you will discover how to make good spiritual choices, and you'll reap the benefits of good spiritual consequences. When you pray, you will discover that nothing is too small for God to care about.

Don't teach the principles of choices and consequences to your family in order to scare them into not doing the wrong thing. Teach it to encourage them to do the right thing.

~

Spectacular things don't happen very often, but the small stuff happens all the time. And when you begin to see God in the small stuff of your family's lives, then they will become spectacular.

*All our life is
a celebration for us,
we are convinced,
in fact, that God is
always everywhere.*

CLEMENT OF ALEXANDRIA

About the Authors

Bruce Bickel is a lawyer and **Stan Jantz** is a marketing consultant. But don't let those mundane occupations fool you. Bruce and Stan have collaborated on fifteen books, with combined sales of more than a million copies. Their passion is to present biblical truth in a clear, correct, and casual manner that encourages people to connect in a meaningful way with the living God.

Bruce and his wife, Cheryl, live in Fresno, California; they are active at Westmont College where Bruce is on the Board of Trustees and their two children attend. Stan and his wife, Karin, also live in Fresno; they are involved at Biola University where Stan is on the Board of Trustees and their two children attend.

Contact Bruce & Stan at:
www.bruceandstan.com

AVAILABLE
WHEREVER BOOKS
ARE SOLD

256 pages each; $12.99